Planning for Learning through Minibeasts

Rachel Sparks Linfield and Penny Coltman   Illustrated by Cathy Hughes

Contents

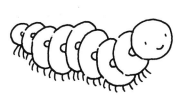

Published by Step Forward Publishing Limited
35 Park Court, Park Street, Leamington Spa CV32 4QN Tel: 01926 420046
© Step Forward Publishing Limited 1999
Planning for Learning through Minibeasts ISBN: 1 902438 124

Making plans

Why plan?

The purpose of planning is to make sure that all children enjoy a broad and balanced curriculum. All planning should be useful. Plans are working documents which you spend time preparing, but which should later repay your efforts. Try to be concise. This will help you in finding information quickly when you need it.

Long-term plans

Preparing a long-term plan, which maps out the curriculum during a year or even two, will help you to ensure that you are providing a variety of activities and are meeting statutory requirements of the Early Learning Goals (1999).

Your long-term plan need not be detailed. Divide the time period over which you are planning into fairly equal sections, such as half terms. Choose a topic for each section. Young children benefit from making links between the new ideas they encounter so as you select each topic, think about the time of year in which you plan to do it. Minibeasts is best covered in the spring or summer rather than the middle of winter.

Although each topic will address all the areas of learning, some could focus on a specific area. For example, a topic on Colour would lend itself well to activities relating to knowledge and understanding of the world and creative areas. Another topic might particularly encourage the appreciation of stories. Try to make sure that you provide a variety of topics in your long-term plans.

Autumn 1	Colour
Autumn 2	Autumn/Christmas
Spring 1	Fairy stories
Spring 2	Shapes
Summer 1	Toys
Summer 2	Minibeasts

Medium-term plans

Medium-term plans will outline the contents of a topic in a little more detail. One way to start this process is by brainstorming on a large piece of paper. Work with your team writing down all the activities you can think of which are relevant to the topic. As you do this it may become clear that some activities go well together. Think about dividing them into themes. Minibeasts, for example, has themes such as 'Hum and buzz', 'Flutter and fly', 'Creep and crawl' and 'Minibeast world'.

At this stage it is helpful to make a chart. Write the theme ideas down the side of the chart and put a different area of learning at the top of each column. Now you can insert your brainstormed ideas and quickly see where there are gaps. As you complete the chart take account of children's earlier experiences and provide opportunities for them to progress.

Refer back to the Early Learning Goals document and check that you have addressed as many different aspects of it as you can. Once all your medium-term plans are complete make sure that there are no neglected areas.

Day-to-day plans

The plans you make for each day will outline aspects such as:

● resources needed;

● the way in which you might introduce activities;

● the organisation of adult help;

● size of the group;

● timing.

Identify the learning which each activity is intended to promote. Make a note of any assessments or observations which you are likely to carry out. On your plans make notes of which activities were particularly successful, or any changes you would make another time.

A final note

Planning should be seen as flexible. Not all groups meet every day, and not all children attend every day. Any part of the plan can be used independently, stretched over a longer period or condensed to meet the needs of any group. You will almost certainly adapt the activities as children respond to them in different ways and bring their own ideas, interests and enthusiasms. Be prepared to be flexible over timing as some ideas prove more popular than others. The important thing is to ensure that the children are provided with a varied and enjoyable curriculum which meets their individual developing needs.

Making plans

Using the book

- Collect or prepare suggested resources as listed on page 21.

- Read the section which outlines links to the Early Learning Goals (pages 4 - 7) and explains the rationale for the topic of Minibeasts.

- For each weekly theme, at least two activities are described in detail as an example to help you in your planning and preparation. Key vocabulary, questions and learning opportunities are identified.

- The skills chart on page 23 will help you to see at a glance which aspects of children's development are being addressed as a focus each week.

- As children take part in the Minibeast topic activities, their learning will progress. 'Collecting evidence' on page 22 explains how you might monitor children's achievements.

- Find out on page 20 how the topic can be brought together in a grand finale involving parents, children and friends.

- There is additional material to support the working partnership of families and children in the form of a 'Home links' page, and a photocopiable 'Parent's page' found at the back of the book.

It is important to appreciate that the ideas presented in this book will only be a part of your planning. Many activities which will be taking place as routine in your group may not be mentioned. For example, it is assumed that sand, dough, water, puzzles, floor toys and large scale apparatus are part of the ongoing pre-school experience. Many groups will also be able to provide access to computers and other aspects of information and communication technology. Role play areas, stories, rhymes and singing, and group discussion times are similarly assumed to be happening each week although they may not be a focus for described activities.

Using the Early Learning Goals

Having decided on your topic and made your medium-term plans you can use the Early Learning Goals to highlight the key learning opportunities your activities will address. The Early Learning Goals are split into six areas: Personal, Social and Emotional Development, Language and Literacy, Mathematics, Knowledge and Understanding of the World, Physical Development and Creative Development. Do not expect each of your topics to cover every goal but your long-term plans should allow for each child to work towards all of the goals.

The following section highlights parts of the Early Learning Goals document in point form to show what children are expected to be able to do by the time they enter Year 1 in each area of learning. These points will be used throughout this book to show how activities for a topic on Minibeasts link to these expectations. For example, Personal, Social and Emotional Development point 8 is 'work as part of a group or class taking turns'. Activities suggested which provide the opportunity for children to do this will have the reference PS8. This will enable you to see which parts of the Early Learning Goals are covered in a given week and plan for areas to be revisited and developed.

In addition you can ensure that activities offer variety in the outcomes to be encountered. Often a similar activity may be carried out to achieve different outcomes. For example, during this topic children make jointed caterpillars to pull along. They will be learning how to use simple tools and equipment to make a moving model but they will also be exploring shape in three dimensions and using their imagination. It is important therefore that activities have clearly defined learning outcomes so that these may be emphasised during the activity and for recording purposes.

Personal, Social and Emotional Development (PS)

This area of learning incorporates attitudes, skills and understanding and is a pre-condition for children's success in all other learning. The goals include children's personal, social, emotional, moral and spiritual development and the establishment of good attitudes to their learning.

By the end of the reception year most children should be:

PS1 confident to try things, initiate ideas and speak in a group

PS2 able to maintain attention, concentrate and sit still

PS3 interested, excited and motivated to learn

PS4 aware of their own needs, views and feelings and sensitive to the needs, views and feelings of others

PS5 respectful of their own cultures and beliefs and those of other people

PS6 responsive to significant experiences showing a range of feelings including joy, awe, wonder and sorrow

They should be able to:

PS7 form good relationships with peers and adults

PS8 work as a part of a group or class taking turns and sharing fairly; understanding that there need to be agreed values and codes of behaviour for groups of people, including adults and children, to work harmoniously

PS9 understand what is right, what is wrong and why

PS10 dress and undress independently and manage their own personal hygiene

PS11 select and use activities and resources independently

PS12 consider the consequences of their words and actions for themselves and others

PS13 understand that people have different needs, views, cultures and beliefs which need to be treated with respect

The topic of Minibeasts offers many opportunities for children's personal, social and emotional development. As children learn more of the small creatures around them, so they will gain respect for their environment. They will discuss aspects such as the need to treat small animals with care and gentleness, causing as little disturbance as possible, as they explore. By playing circle games children will learn to take turns and to understand the need for agreed codes of behaviour. Many of the areas outlined above, though, will be covered on an almost incidental basis as children carry out the activities described for the other areas of learning. During undirected free choice times they will be developing independence (PS 11) whilst any small group activity which involves working with an adult will help children to build effective relationships (PS 7).

Language and Literacy (L)

These goals are in line with the National Literacy Strategy.

Speaking and Listening

By the end of the reception year, most children should be able to:

L1 use language to imagine and recreate roles and experiences

L2 use talk to organise, sequence and clarify thinking, ideas, feelings and events

L3 sustain attentive listening, responding to what they have heard by relevant comments, questions or actions

L4 interact with others negotiating plans and activities and taking turns in conversation

L5 extend their vocabulary exploring the meaning and sounds of new words

L6 retell narratives in the correct sequence drawing on the language pattern of stories

L7 speak clearly and audibly with confidence and control and show awareness of the listener, for example by their use of conventions such as greetings, 'please' and 'thank you'

Reading

By the end of reception most children should be able to:

L8 hear and say initial and final sounds in words and short vowel sounds within words

L9 link letters and sounds, naming and sounding all letters of the alphabet

L10 read a range of familiar and common words and simple sentences independently

L11 show understanding of elements of stories such as main character, sequence of events, opening and how information can be found in non-fiction texts, to answer questions about where, who, why and how

Writing

By the end of reception most children should be able to:

L12 hold a pencil correctly, and form recognisable letters, most of which are correctly formed

L13 use their phonic knowledge to write simple regular words and make phonetically plausible attempts at more complex words

L14 write their own names and labels and form sentences, sometimes using punctuation

L15 Attempt writing for various purposes, using features of different forms such as lists, stories, instructions

The activities suggested for the theme of Minibeasts include several which are based on well-known, quality picture books and stories. They allow children to enjoy listening to the books and to respond in a variety of ways to what they hear, reinforcing and extending their vocabularies. Throughout the topic opportunities are described in which children are encouraged to explore the sounds of words, to use descriptive vocabulary and to see some of their ideas recorded in both pictures and words.

Mathematics (M)

These goals reflect the key objectives in the National Numeracy Strategy.

By the end of reception most children should be able to:

M1 say and use number names in order in familiar contexts

M2 count reliably up to ten everyday objects

M3 recognise numerals 1 to 9

M4 use language such as 'more' or 'less', 'greater' or 'smaller', 'heavier' or 'lighter' to compare two numbers or quantities

M5 in practical activities and discussion begin to use the vocabulary involved in adding and subtracting

M6 find one more or one less than a number from one to ten

M7 begin to relate addition to combining two groups of objects and subtraction to 'taking away'

M8 talk about, recognise and recreate simple patterns

M9 use language such as 'circle' or 'bigger' to describe the shape and size of solids and flat shapes

M10 use everyday words to describe position

M11 use developing mathematical ideas and methods to solve practical problems

The theme of Minibeasts provides opportunities for a range of mathematical activities presented in meaningful and practical contexts. A number of them allow children to develop sorting and counting skills. Children are given the opportunity to develop early understandings of addition and subtraction, and to begin to explore aspects of measure.

Knowledge and Understanding of the World (K)

These goals provide a foundation for scientific, technological, historical and geographical learning.

By the end of reception most children should be able to:

K1 investigate objects and materials by using all of their senses as appropriate

K2 find out about and identify some features of living things, objects and events they observe

K3 look closely at similarities, differences, patterns and change

K4 ask questions about why things happen and how things work

K5 build and construct with a wide range of objects, selecting appropriate resources and adapting their work where necessary

K6 select tools and techniques they need to shape, assemble and join the materials they are using

K7 find out about and identify the uses of technology in their everyday lives and use computers and programmed toys to support their learning

K8 find out about past and present events in their own lives, and those of their families and other people they know

K9 observe, find out about and identify features in the place where they live and the natural world

K10 find out about their environment and talk about those features they like and dislike

The topic of Minibeasts offers many opportunities for children to explore and investigate, to make observations and to ask questions. They can extend their awareness of the local environment as they search for minibeasts and discover different habitats. They will learn more about the variety of minibeasts around them and begin to know something of the similarities and differences between them.

Physical Development (PD)

By the end of reception most children should be able to:

PD1 move with confidence, imagination and in safety

PD2 move with control and co-ordination

PD3 show awareness of space, of themselves and of others

PD4 recognise the importance of keeping healthy and those things which contribute to this

PD5 recognise the changes that happen to their bodies when they are active

PD6 use a range of small and large equipment

PD7 travel around, under, over and through balancing and climbing equipment

PD8 handle tools, objects, construction and malleable materials safely with increasing control

Activities such as working with dough and preparing food will offer experience of PD8. Through imitating the actions of minibeasts and enacting life-cycles children will have the opportunity to develop the skills of moving with confidence and imagination. Opportunities are taken to encourage control as children play games of throwing and aiming, and more active games give opportunities for adults to draw children's attention to changes in their bodies.

Creative Development (C)

By the end of reception most children should be able to:

C1 explore colour, texture, shape, form and space in two and three dimensions

C2 listen attentively to and explore how sounds can be made louder/quieter, faster/slower, longer/shorter, higher/lower and recognise patterns in music, movement and dance

C3 respond in a variety of ways to what they see, hear, smell, touch and feel

C4 use their imagination in art and design, music, dance, drama, stories and play

C5 express and communicate their ideas, thoughts and feelings by using a widening range of materials, suitable tools, drama, movement, designing and making, and a variety of songs and instruments

During this topic children will experience working with a variety of materials as they weave, make models, and explore a range of creative making tasks. Music is used as a way of supporting imaginative movement, with suggestions for the use of pitch, tempo and volume. Throughout all the activities children are encouraged to talk about what they see and feel as they communicate their ideas in 2D and 3D work, dance, music and role play.

Week 1

Meet the minibeasts!

Personal, Social and Emotional Development

- Start by taking the children on a minibeast walk (see activity opposite). Discuss aspects of safety, such as the need to hold hands or for the group to stay together. Draw attention to any hazards such as roads or ponds and explain the safety rules associated with them. (PS12)

- Ask the children to imagine they are tiny minibeasts. What sort of thing might frighten them? Talk about the importance of behaving as 'gentle giants' when working with such small animals. (PS6)

Language and Literacy

- Make journey sticks to record the walk. The adult accompanying each group of children needs a strip of card, about 3 x 10 cm. Place a piece of double-sided adhesive tape down the centre of the card. At various stages along the walk the group then chooses a tiny memento to fix to the card: a piece of grass from the footpath, a tiny white flower from the bush near the park gate, and so on. (If the adult is in charge of the card, it avoids the risk of children collecting living creatures!) Afterwards, use the journey sticks as a focus for discussion, describing the walk and placing events in sequence. (L2, 6)

- Encourage the children to talk about the minibeasts they found on their walk. Use prepositions - on the wall, under the stone, between the blades of grass. (L5)

- Encourage recognition of initial sounds by playing a game of 'I spied', referring to minibeasts seen on the walk. For example, 'I spied, with my little eye, a minibeast beginning with 'c'.' (L8)

Mathematics

- Talk about the idea of being very small. What other things can the children think of which are very small? Encourage them to make comparisons. Can you think of something in this room which is about as big as a ladybird? (M4)

- Provide a selection of plastic minibeasts for children to arrange in order of size. Which has the longest legs? Which is the smallest? (M4)

- Use the plastic minibeasts for counting activities. Start with a small group of minibeasts and show the children how to count them, touching each in turn and moving it to one side. Progress to counting with touching but not moving. Provide numerals for more able or older children to use in recording the count of each set. (M1, 2, 3)

Knowledge and Understanding of the World

- Go on a minibeast walk (see activity opposite). (K2)

- After the walk, ask children to describe the animals they saw, referring to colour, size, legs, wings or shell. See if they can sort plastic minibeasts using their own chosen criteria. (K3)

- Talk to the children about their own experiences of minibeasts. Ask them to think of recent events such as finding a spider in the bath! (K8)

Physical Development

- Make an obstacle course in which children move as minibeasts through an imaginary world. Include tunnels (worm holes) to travel through, benches (twigs and branches) to balance along, cones (stones) to move between and mats (leaves) to rest on. Clap to give a danger signal of an approaching hungry bird, at which all the 'minibeasts' must freeze to avoid being spotted! (PD1, 2, 3, 6, 7)

- Place a selection of plastic minibeasts on the dough table so that children can use them as inspiration as they model their own. (PD8)

Creative Development

- Use a variety of percussion instruments to produce sounds to which children move like minibeasts. Shake a tambourine to suggest wriggling or slithering. Use gentle triangle sounds for fluttering butterflies, a swanee whistle for leaping grasshoppers and maracas for scuttling beetles. (C3, 4)

- Make a minibeast tree role play area (see activity opposite). (C5)

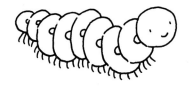

Activity: The minibeast walk

Learning opportunity: Developing an awareness of the minibeasts to be found in the immediate environment.

Early Learning Goal: Knowledge and Understanding of the World. Children should find out about and identify some features of living things, objects and events they observe.

Resources: Adult helpers, preferably one to every two or three children; magnifiers.

Key vocabulary: Insect, worm, slug, snail, woodlouse, spider, wings, legs.

Organisation: Whole group.

Note: Unless you have access to a fairly large enclosed outdoor space for your group, such as school grounds, you will need to consult your policy regarding trips and outings. You will need written parental consent before taking children out of the group's premises.

What to do:

Divide your walk into distinct stages, each of which focuses on a different type of habitat, for example grassy area, hedgerow, stone pile, rotting logs, old wall. At each place stop and encourage the children to look for minibeasts, using the magnifiers to help them to see tiny detail. Talk about searching at different levels, looking behind and under objects. Many minibeasts prefer dark, damp environments, so carefully lifting away a piece of bark from an old log is often fruitful. When searching hedgerows remember to look under leaves as well as on their surfaces. Talk about camouflage - some animals are hard to spot!

Discourage the children from touching or collecting their finds. Small animals are easily damaged by handling and some, especially woodlice, will quickly die if they are kept away from their damp habitats.

Record the findings of your walk by photographs which can later be displayed.

Activity: Minibeast tree role play area

Learning opportunity: Working collaboratively, using a variety of materials, tools and techniques in building an imaginative play area.

Early Learning Goal: Creative Development. Children should express and communicate their ideas ..... using a widening range of materials and suitable tools.

Resources: String or thin wire; green crepe paper in various shades; paint; large brushes; green paper; card; glue; scissors; travelling rug; picnic basket and accessories.

Key vocabulary: Cut, paint, minibeasts, picnic.

Organisation: Small groups contributing, one at a time

What to do:

Make space in the corner of the room where you want the area to be. Make a backdrop by covering the walls either side of the corner with white backing paper. Cut out a tree trunk shape which will reach from floor to ceiling for children to paint. Mount it in the corner between the two walls. A second group of children can cut out leaf shapes from green paper. Add these to the top of the tree.

Next make a leafy curtain through which children will enter the area. Fix two hooks in the ceiling or the top of the walls, about 1.5 m away from the corner. If possible put a third hook in the ceiling so that a 'square' is formed , the four corners of which are the top of the corner of the room, and the three hooks. Fix a line of tight string or fine wire like a washing line between the three hooks. Two sides of the square are now the walls, and two are the line.

Show a group of children how to make crepe paper twists. Cut all the way across unopened rolls of green crepe paper at 2 cm intervals. Twist these unopened strips tightly, then shake them out to make green streamers. Hang them from the suspended line to form a green curtain which resembles the dangling branches of a weeping willow tree. Trim the lengths of paper so that the branches hang just above the floor.

Place a picnic rug and accessories on the floor inside the 'tree'. Let children cut out their own drawings of minibeasts and stick them to the leaves, trunk and dangling branches. Details such as fringed paper grass or card flowers will give further ideas for creatures to include.

Display

Make a display of the photographs taken on the minibeast walk. Let the children help you compose suitable captions. These will prompt the children to talk about their experiences as they share the pictures with group visitors. Include examples of the journey sticks.

Week 2

Week 2 Creep and crawl

Personal, Social and Emotional Development

- Introduce the idea of creeping and crawling as examples of slow movement. Is it better to move quickly? Sometimes when we are in a hurry we forget things or make mistakes. Talk about times when we need to hurry. (PS2, 12)

- Re-tell the story of the tortoise and the hare but change the central characters to a snail and a centipede. Centipedes have so many legs that they are unable to run very quickly and the steady pace of the snail wins the day. (PS 12)

Language and Literacy

- Say together this traditional action rhyme (L3):

Underneath a stone where the soil was firm

(One hand makes a 'fist' stone)

I found a wiggly, wiggly worm.

(Tip the fist stone to reveal a wriggling finger from the other hand)

'Good morning,' I said, and 'How are you today?'
(Talk to wriggling finger)

But the wiggly worm just wriggled away.

(Finger wriggles behind back)

- Talk about the words ' wiggly worm'. They both begin with the same sound. Can the children identify the sound? Offer the children some other minibeast word pairs: slithering slugs, beautiful butterflies, snoozing snails, colourful caterpillars. In each case ask them to identify the initial sound. (L8)

Mathematics

- Use woollen worms as a unit of non-standard measure (see activity opposite). (M4)

- Draw and cut out snail shells which are divided into equal sized sections for children to colour in a repeating pattern. Add them to your display. (M 8)

Knowledge and Understanding of the World

- Make trails and patterns in wet clay on a black plastic bin liner. Develop vocabulary as children describe the texture of the clay and its feel against the plastic, and talk about the patterns they make. (K1)

- Make a display of made worms. Choose one or more adjectives to describe the texture of a worm. Give the children large cut-out worm shapes and a selection of appropriate materials. Each worm is covered with scraps to illustrate the chosen adjective. Older or more able children can choose one of a selection of adjectives: a sparkly worm, a smooth worm, a woolly worm, a rough worm. Provide a wider selection of materials for more able children to encourage discrimination. Talk about the choices made and the finished textures of the worms. Display the worms with each one labelled appropriately. (K2)

Physical Development

- Play a version of 'What's the time, Mr Wolf?' The children, pretending to be slugs and snails, edge forwards calling 'What's the time, Mr Thrush?' You stand at the far end of the space with your back to them and say a time: 'One o' clock', 'Two o'clock' and so on. Once you decide that it is 'Dinner time!' you turn around quickly and chase all the minibeasts back to the start. If one of the slugs or snails manages to creep up on you and tap your shoulder, then that child has the next turn at being Mr Thrush. (PD3)

- Use playground chalk to draw long wiggly worm shapes on the ground for children to balance along, or to move along in different ways; hopping, skipping carefully walking backwards. Alternatively place long skipping ropes on the floor indoors to use in the same way. (PD1, 2)

Creative Development

- Make model snails from pasta shells with cut-out paper bodies. (C1, 4)

- Talk about moving quickly and slowly to music. Use a percussion instrument to play notes in alternating quick and slow succession. Invite children to move around the room being a snail or a centipede accordingly. (C2)

- Make a model home for a snail (see activity opposite). (C 1, 4)

Activity: Measuring worms

Learning opportunity: Exploring aspects of linear measure.

Early Learning Goal: Mathematics. Children should use language such as 'more' or 'less' ... to compare quantities.

Resources: Lengths of wool cut as follows (each length of wool should be a different colour): 2 cm, 10 cm, 50 cm, 1 m.

Key vocabulary: Longer than, shorter than, about as long as.

Organisation: Small group.

What to do:

Show the children the cut lengths of wool. Explain that these are special measuring worms. The children are going to use them to measure the lengths of objects in the room. Start by looking at the measuring worms. Which are the shortest and longest? Can the children rank the worms in order from shortest to longest?

Look at the shortest worm. Can the children find anything in the room which is about as long as this worm? Encourage them to move around the room searching for suitable objects. As the collection is assembled discuss how each object compares in length to the worm. Is it about the same length, shorter or longer?

Repeat with the longer worms. Which is the shortest object the children have found during the activity? Which is the longest?

Display some of the objects found next to the worms of corresponding length.

Activity: A home for a snail

Learning opportunity: Working imaginatively with a variety of tools and materials.

Early Learning Goal: Creative Development. Children should use their imagination as they explore colour, texture, shape and form.

Resources: Shopping catalogues; grey and white paper; glue; scissors.

Key vocabulary: Cut, stick, snail, shell, home.

Organisation: Small group.

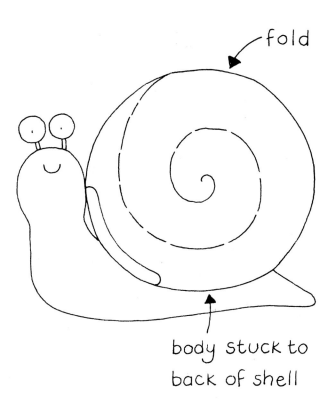

fold

body stuck to back of shell

What to do:

Before the activity prepare a snail for each child as follows:

Cut a large body shape from grey paper (about 30 x 10 cm). Next fold a piece of A3 paper in half and from it cut two identical snail shell shapes joined down the fold line.

Give each child a snail body and a folded paper shell. Show the children how to glue the shell to the body so that it will flap open to show the inside of the shell.

Explain that the shell is the snail's home. What do the children think that the snail would like to have in its home? Invite the children to equip the snail's home either by drawing their own pictures, or by cutting them out of the shopping catalogue and gluing them into place.

Display

Display the snail home designs on a large board. Use captions to invite visitors or other children to guess what each snail has inside its shell. Open the shell flaps to reveal the surprises inside.

Week 3

Hum and buzz

Personal, Social and Emotional Development

- Read the story 'Honey Bee's Busy Day' by Richard Fowler (Doubleday). Talk about the work done by bees as they fly from flower to flower collecting nectar to make honey. When do the children work hard? What about the adults they know? What jobs can children help with? (PS4)

- As the children enjoy their honey sandwiches (see activity opposite), explain how bees work together. They live in groups and share the honey they make. Discuss how by helping each other and working together the children can achieve things which they could not do alone. (PS8)

Language and Literacy

- Make a simple bee-shaped finger puppet by fixing a cut-out bee to a paper band. Introduce your finger puppet as a bee who likes to collect things which begin with the sound 'b'. Encourage the children to identify objects around them which begin with this sound, and then to think of other examples - animals, objects at home. Invite children to record their ideas with drawings, each of which can be cut out and stuck to a small bee-shaped silhouette for display. (L8)

- We describe the noise which bees make as a hum or a buzz. Make a collection of other words which describe animal sounds. (L5)

Mathematics

- Make a collection of cut-out flower shapes. Encourage counting as children take a paper bee for a flight, visiting the flowers, counting as they go. Use a set of 1 to 5 numeral cards. Let children in turn pick a card, identify the numeral and take their bee on a tour of that number of flowers. Include some cards with spots for children to count. More able or older children may work with numbers to ten. (M1, 2, 3)

- Show the children some pictures of honeycomb, or even better, a jar of honey containing a honeycomb. Point out the hexagon shape of the cells in the comb and how they all fit neatly together. Provide plastic pattern blocks, or regular hexagons cut from coloured paper, for children to fit together. (M8, 9, 10)

Knowledge and Understanding of the World

- Make honey sandwiches (see activity opposite). (K1)

- Talk about the children's experiences of bees and wasps. Explain to the children that bees and wasps are small and could easily be damaged by people. Their stings are their way of protecting themselves. (K2, 8)

- Make balloon bees. Partially blow up some round yellow balloons. Provide strips of black paper which can be stuck around the balloon, using PVA glue, to make the stripes. Dark coloured pipe-cleaners can be taped into place for antennae and legs. Show children how to twist white crepe or tissue paper to make the two pairs of wings, and add black paper circle eyes. (K2)

Physical Development

- Play the bee game (see activity opposite). (PD1, 3)

- Use coloured hoops to represent flowers on the floor. See if the children can toss bean bag 'bees' onto the flowers. Vary the size of the hoops, and gradually encourage the children to throw from a greater distance. (PD2, 6)

Creative Development

- Use finger paint to print yellow finger spots on black paper. Show the children how to use white paint to add wings to their finger paint bees. (C1)

- Pre-cut weaving frames from black card. Provide a selection of yellow weaving materials from which children can make choices: strips of different types of yellow paper, foils, parcel ribbon, fabrics, raffia, and so on. (C1, 5)

Activity: Honey sandwiches

Learning opportunity: Exploring aspects of taste and texture.

Early Learning Goal: Knowledge and Understanding of the World. Children should investigate objects and materials by using all of their senses as appropriate.

Resources: A selection of sliced breads; preferably two types of honey (clear and set); butter or

margarine (easy to spread); paper plates; safe knives; teaspoons for tasting honey; clean damp cloth for wiping sticky hands.

Key vocabulary: Sweet, sticky, clear, see-through, cloudy, runny, set, spread, crumbly, brown, white, slice, crust.

Organisation: Small group.

What to do:

Note: As with any tasting activity it is always advisable to check with parents that no children have relevant allergies.

Explain to the children that they are going to make sandwiches to have with their snack. First they are going to make some choices about their sandwiches.

Have one plate of pre-cut tiny squares of the different sliced breads for children to taste. Encourage them to talk about the different textures. Compare the colours. Taste is difficult for children to describe, but they should be encouraged to talk about preferences and may, for example, be able to identify some breads as sweeter than others.

Introduce the types of honey, letting each child taste small quantities using a clean teaspoon. Discuss the appearance of the honey and its pouring qualities.

As you make the sandwiches talk about the thickness of the bread slices, how much butter is needed, and how to spread it to the edges of the bread. Once the honey is added encourage the children to line up the top slice of bread to match the lower one before pressing into place. Cut into triangles or squares.

Activity: The bee game

Learning opportunity: Moving imaginatively and following instructions.

Early Learning Goal: Physical Development. Children should move with confidence, imagination and in safety.

Resources: Bean bags; coloured hoops; long rope or marker cones; large space.

Key vocabulary: Pollen, hive, flower, queen bee.

Organisation: Whole group.

What to do:

This game is a variation on the 'Port and Starboard' game popular in Cub and Brownie groups.

The children are going to pretend to be bees. Use the long rope or marker cones to mark out a large area. This is the hive. Scatter at least one bean bag per child around the space. These represent the pollen which the bees collect. Place the coloured hoops on the floor as flowers for the bees to visit. Choose an adult to be the queen bee of the colony.

Explain to the children that they are going to 'fly' around the large space to the accompaniment of some suitable music or the shaking of a tambourine. When the sound stops you are going to give them an instruction to follow.

Go home to the hive: Children move to the hive area.

Collect pollen: Each child finds a bean bag and stands still holding it.

Visit the queen bee: Children move to the designated adult and stand around them.

Find a flower: Each child stands in a hoop.

Sleeping bees: Children lie on the floor.

Buzzing bees: Children spin around on the spot making a buzzing noise.

Display

Make a display of the balloon bees made by the children with examples of their weavings. Place a jar of honey with some picture books about bees on a table in front of the display.

Week 4

Flutter and fly

Personal, Social and Emotional Development

- Read the story book *If at First You Do Not See ...* by Ruth Brown (Scholastic). This book, which tells the story of a caterpillar's adventures, contains pictures which appear differently when the book is held upside down. Encourage children to take turns in guessing what the upside down picture might look like. (PS 1, 2, 3, 8)

- Talk about how fragile butterflies are and the need to handle them as little as possible, but if necessary with extreme care. Hold a 'careful handling challenge': pass a bell or a bunch of keys around a circle of children. Can they pass it without making a sound? (PS 4, 6)

Language and Literacy

- Sing together the following traditional action song which uses the tune of 'Twinkle Twinkle Little Star'. Say the words slowly and distinctly enjoying the sounds they make:

Little Arabella Millar,

(Hold one arm straight and start to wiggle the forefinger from the other hand slowly up it)

Found a woolly caterpillar,

(Continue the wiggling)

First she put it on her mother,

Then upon her baby brother.

They said 'Arabella Millar,

Take away that caterpillar!'

(Adopt a cross voice and pretend to brush the caterpillar off the outstretched arm.) (L5)

- Give each child as many pre-cut paper circles as there are letters in their name. Show the children how to arrange the circles to make a caterpillar. The first circle is the caterpillar's head. Scribe the child's initial onto this. Subsequent letters are written on each of the following circles. Adapt for each child - some may be able to write independently, some to copy, some to join dots. Decorate them with paint or collage patterns and add short lengths of pipe-cleaner for legs. Make a display of name caterpillars. (L 14)

Mathematics

- Make a set of ladybirds from circles of red card to use for counting activities (see activity opposite). (M1, 2)

- Prepare a number of butterflies cut from thin card. Decorate each one with symmetrical wing patterns. Cut each butterfly in half, down the centre of its body. Spread the half butterflies on the table and see if children can find the matching pairs of wings. (M8)

Knowledge and Understanding of the World

- Make jointed caterpillars to pull along (see activity opposite). (K5, 6)

- Illustrate the butterfly's life-cycle using playdough. Start with an egg-shaped piece of dough. As the caterpillar hatches from the egg, pull the dough into a long caterpillar shape. Press it into a short, fat pupa and, finally, mould an adult butterfly. (K2, 3)

Physical Development

- Encourage the children to model shapes from the butterfly life-cycle. (PD8)

- Lay a series of cones, hoops or mats for the children to move between as they fly around a large space. (PD1, 2, 3)

Creative Development

- Use music to direct the movement of children as they work in the role of flying insects. Use high notes to denote moving on tiptoes with wings held high, and low notes for flying nearer to the ground with lowered wings, similarly fast and slow sequences of notes to tell children at what speed they should be flying. (C2)

- Make butterfly leaf pictures. Each child needs a flat shape rolled from an egg-sized piece of clay. Make sure that the clay is damp but not too wet. Provide a selection of leaves, large petals and small pieces of twig. Show the children how to press the materials into the clay to make simple pictures. Lift the finished pieces of work onto card to display or take home. (C1, 4, 5)

Activity: Number ladybirds

Learning opportunity: Developing counting skills.

Early Learning Goal: Mathematics. Children should count reliably up to ten everyday objects.

Resources: Ladybird shapes (without spots) made from circles of red card, flat round pebbles or safe jar lids painted with red ready-mixed paint to which a little PVA glue has been added; black paint; brushes; PVA glue.

Key vocabulary: Number names from one to ten.

Organisation: Small group.

What to do:

Paint a black head onto each shape and then draw a black line down the centre of each, denoting the two wings. (Adding about half a teaspoon of PVA glue to ready-mixed paint will help the paint to coat a shiny surface and prevent it from flaking.) Involve the children in helping you to transform the red, round shapes into ladybirds by adding the black spots to each wing, counting them as they do so.

Once the ladybirds are complete use them for a variety of number activities. Can you make a line of five ladybirds? Add one more ladybird to the line. How many are there now? Can you find two ladybirds with the same number of spots? Make one of your ladybirds fly away. How many are there now?

Activity: Jointed caterpillars

Learning opportunity: Using simple tools and equipment to make a moving model.

Early Learning Goal: Creative Development. Children should use suitable tools in designing and making.

Resources: Card cylinders (about 10 cm long); a single hole punch; plenty of treasury tags; pipe-cleaners; paints and brushes; decorative materials and glue.

Key vocabulary: Join, move, cut, stick.

Organisation: Small group.

What to do:

Make two holes at each end of each cylinder. The holes should be opposite each other and as near as possible to the cylinder ends. This is best done with a single hole punch, but can be done by an adult by resting the cylinder on a soft surface and pressing through a pointed object.

Show the children how to join two cylinders by threading treasury tags through the holes at their ends. The cylinders are now held together but can move quite freely.

Encourage each child to make a caterpillar of four or five cylinders using this technique. Paint and decorative materials can be used to finish the model, with pipe-cleaner antennae added to the head. Tie a string to the head so that the caterpillar can be pulled along with a satisfying wriggling action!

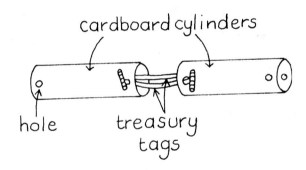

cardboard cylinders

hole   treasury tags

Display

Prepare a background of green paper grass and bright flowers made from coloured crepe paper. Display the name caterpillars crawling though the grass, and the collage butterflies fluttering amongst the flowers. Add key words such as butterfly, caterpillar, crawl, wings, flutter and fly.

Week 5
Weave and spin

Personal, Social and Emotional Development

- Some children are afraid of spiders. Read the story of *Molly and the Snorgle Fly* by Satoshi Kambayashi (Tesco Books). Molly is afraid of insects until the magical snorgle fly reduces her to their size and she discovers a surprisingly friendly world. (PS 4)

- Children are fascinated by spiders' webs. Go looking for them outside, especially on a damp, dewy morning or a frosty day, and marvel at the work that has gone into making such wonderful creations. (PS 6)

Language and Literacy

- Enjoy rhymes which have spider connections: 'Incy Wincy Spider' and 'Little Miss Muffet'. Encourage joining in with actions or by acting out the roles of Miss Muffet and the spider.(L3)

- Tell the children stories of Anancy. Anancy stories come from the Caribbean and can be found in a number of anthologies, including *Listen to this Story* by Grace Hallworth. Anancy, a cunning and lively character who loves to play tricks, is known as the spider man because he is able to change from man to spider and back again. (L3)

Mathematics

- Make a spider board game (see activity opposite). (M11)

- Make model spiders from egg-box bumps painted black. Encourage the children to count the eight pipe-cleaner legs as they are added. Dangle the spiders on pieces of wool. Whose spider is on the longest thread? Whose is on the shortest? Hang the spiders around the room and ask questions to introduce positional language. Who can see the spider between the books and the window? Can you see a spider under a table? (M 1, 4, 10)

Knowledge and Understanding of the World

- Provide children with fairly substantial branched twigs and encourage them to wind wool around them, making a simple web. Take the children outside and encourage them to make collections of natural materials to catch in their webs;

attractive leaves, petals, feathers, grasses. Talk about the different collections the children have made and where they made their finds. If you want to carry out the activity indoors, let children choose from a wide selection of decorative materials to add to their webs. (K5, 9)

- Make fridge magnet spiders (see activity opposite). (K4)

Physical Development

- Encourage the children to move on two hands and two feet in a spider-like manner. At a signal the spiders must roll into a tight ball and freeze to avoid danger. (PD1)

- Chalk a large web of three large circles, one inside each other on the ground. Mark a centre spot and add radiating lines to complete the web effect. One child stands in the centre as the spider. The remaining children are flies, standing on the innermost circle of the web. A bean bag is repeatedly tossed between the spider in the middle and the flies around. Children who catch the bean bag step onto the next outer circle, until they eventually escape from the web. This child now becomes the spider and the game starts again. (PD 2, 6)

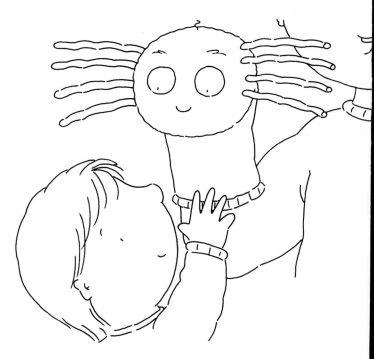

Creative Development

- Cut notches around the outside edge of a black card circle. Prepare weaving frames by repeatedly winding wool across the circle to make 'spokes'. Supply the children with long lengths of ribbon or strips of crepe paper. Help by fixing one end to the centre of the frame and then show the children how to weave in an outward spiral, around and around the web. (C 1)

- Make spider finger puppets. The paper puppets have six legs and the fingers form the final two. Use the finger puppets as children carry out actions to accompany 'Incy Wincy Spider'. (C4)

Activity: Spider board game

Learning opportunity: Developing strategies to solve a puzzle.

Early Learning Goal: Mathematics. Children should use mathematical ideas and methods to solve practical problems. (M11)

Resources: Large square cut from an A3 piece of card; a few paper 'flies'; a small plastic or card spider; two dice, each marked 1, 1, 2, 2, 3, 3.

Key vocabulary: Number names one to three, forwards, backwards, sideways.

Organisation: One or two players.

What to do:

Mark the board into squares, about 5 x 5 cm. Draw a simple spider web pattern to cover the whole of the board. Laminate the board or cover with self-adhesive clear film to protect it.

Dot a few of the paper flies, randomly, in squares around the board. The spider is placed at the centre of the web. The children then take turns to throw both dice. They can move the spider the number of counts on the dice in any direction. For example, if the throw is 2, 3, the player could move two squares up and three across, or five squares in one direction.

The object of the game is to collect the flies from the board. If more than one child is playing, the winner is the person who has collected the most flies at the end of the game. Simplify the game for younger or less able children by throwing just one dice and allowing that number of moves in one or more chosen directions.

Activity: Fridge magnet spiders

Learning opportunity: Exploring aspects of magnetism.

Early Learning Goal: Knowledge and Understanding of the World. Children should ask questions about why things happen and how things work. (K4)

Resources: Small button magnets (available from craft shops) or short (1 cm) lengths of magnetic strip (from an educational suppliers); black card circles; black paper; sequins; scissors; glue.

Key vocabulary: Magnet, attract.

Organisation: Small group.

What to do:

Show the children how to make simple model spiders by adding black paper legs and sequin eyes to their card circles. Each spider is then glued onto a button magnet or piece of magnetic strip.

Use the spider magnets to explore aspects of magnetism. Encourage the children to look around the room. Which objects attract the spider magnet? What happens when two spider magnets are put together?

Display

Make a huge woollen web in a corner of the room by fixing strands from either side of a corner to a point in the ceiling at some distance. Knot other threads into the web to complete it. Hang the various spiders which the children have made from the giant web.

Week 6

Minibeast world

Personal, Social and Emotional Development

- Tell the children the fable of 'The Grasshopper and the Ants' (Aesop). The grasshopper preferred to rest and play all summer, whilst the ants busied themselves collecting food for the winter. When winter came the poor grasshopper was hungry. Ask the children to think about whether or not the ants would have helped him and to discuss their ideas. (PS 4, 12)

- Explain to the children that they are going to hold a Minibeast World event to which families and friends can be invited. There is going to be lots to do to prepare for the event and everyone will need to help. (L4)

Language and Literacy

- Show the children some pictures of minibeasts and tell them their names: dragonfly, woodlouse, house fly. Can they think how these creatures came by their names? Show some less common examples, for example photographs of Amazonian butterflies or exotic beetles, and ask the children to make up their own names for them. (L3, 5)

- Tell the story of the minibeast ball (see activity opposite). (L 3)

Mathematics

- Make minibeast hat bands. Start by showing children how to measure around their heads using wool. This will help them in cutting a length of card strip to an appropriate length. Give support in this process. Check if it is long enough. With the card strip laid flat on the table, encourage the children to decorate them with insect designs: red with black spots, grasshopper green with collage materials to give texture, jewelled with gummed shapes. Introduce ideas of repeating patterns and talk about the shapes of different decorative materials. Use bendy drinking straws or pipe-cleaners to make antennae, and then fix the ends together. Provide a safe mirror to admire the results! (M11)

- Make a simple beetle game. Prepare bodies, heads and legs cut from coloured paper. Children take turns to throw a dice labelled either 1, 1, 2, 2, 3, 3 or with equivalent numbers

of spots on each face for younger or less able children. Collect a body when a 1 is thrown, a head for a 2 and a leg for a 3. Only one beetle can be in progress at any one time. (M1, 2, 3)

Knowledge and Understanding of the World

- Make paper plate camouflage masks (see activity opposite). (K5)

- Talk about the places which the children have visited and the minibeasts they saw there. Encourage the children to describe the features they encountered (hedge, wall, path, stones, logs, pond, grass) and to use positional language as they remember their finds (under the stone, behind the bench). (K9)

Physical Development

- Use the following action rhyme to encourage imaginative movement:

  If I was a minibeast

  Guess what I would be.

  I'd like to be a beetle

  (Insert different minibeast names)

  And this is what you'd see ....

  ME! Going .....

  Scuttle and stop, scuttle and stop, scuttle and stop.

Alternative verses might include: butterfly - flutter and fly; worm - wriggle and slide; dragonfly - hover and swoop; snail - creep and crawl.

Invite children to make additional suggestions.

Creative Development

- Either individually or collaboratively, make giant sized models of insects using recycled materials to hang from the ceiling. (C1)

- Use a variety of natural materials to build a home for an imaginary minibeast. (C1, 4)

Activity: The minibeast ball

Learning opportunity: Responding to, and joining in a story-telling activity.

Early Learning Goal: Language and Literacy. Children should sustain attentive listening, responding to what they have heard by relevant .... actions.

Resources: Large space; picture cards (one per child): several of each of a variety of well-known minibeasts such as ladybirds, butterflies, snails, caterpillars, beetles.

Key vocabulary: Names of minibeasts.

Organisation: Whole group sitting in a circle.

What to do:

Explain to the children that you are going to tell them a story about the minibeast ball. They are going to be the minibeasts and help you with the story! Give each child a picture card, such that there is a group of ladybirds, butterflies, caterpillars and so on. The picture cards will help the children to remember which minibeast they are.

Decide on an action for each minibeast. The children will do this action every time their minibeast is mentioned. The caterpillars, for example, might move their arms in a loopy caterpillar crawl action and the butterflies might stand and flutter their wings.

At the start of the story set the scene, introducing each minibeast group one at a time. For example:

'It was the day of the minibeast ball. The caterpillars were given the invitations to deliver. They took them round the garden visiting each minibeast home in turn. The ladybirds were busily repainting the spots on their ball dresses. Meanwhile the snails had set off early so as not to be late ......'

As the children become confident in recognising their minibeast cues, increase the pace of the game by introducing characters more frequently and sometimes repeating them quite quickly.

Activity: Paper plate camouflage masks

Learning opportunity: Making a mask using a range of materials.

Early Learning Goal: Knowledge and Understanding of the World. Children should select tools and techniques they need to shape, assemble and join the materials they are using.

Resources: Sandpaper; sand tray; paper plates (with pre-cut eye holes); leaves; flowers; coloured paper; scissors; glue; covered elastic, ribbon or lolly sticks.

Key vocabulary: Camouflage, hide, colours.

Organisation: Small group.

What to do:

Cut out a shape from sandpaper and place it on the surface of the sand tray. The sandpaper shape is hard to see. Explain to the children that sometimes animals need to hide. Minibeasts, particularly, need to hide from hungry birds who would eat them.

Remind the children of minibeasts they may have found which were hard to spot. Greenfly, for example, are often difficult to see on leaves. Introduce the word 'camouflage' to describe this use of colour and pattern as a way of hiding.

Explain to the children that they are going to make camouflage masks. Draw their attention to an outside area - a hedge, flower bed or some bushes. Show them the paper plates and suggest ways of covering the plate with the materials provided, so that the children could hide in their chosen area without being seen.

Once the plates are covered, attach the covered elastic or ribbons to the sides so that the mask can be held in place. Alternatively fix the plate to a lolly stick so that it can be held in front of the face.

Display

Display the completed masks against a background similar to the chosen area. How difficult are the masks to spot?

Bringing it all together

Introducing the Minibeast World idea

Explain to the children that they are going to invite friends and families to join them for a special event. They will be enjoying minibeast activities together, and showing some of the work they have been doing.

Encourage the children to think about some of the activities they have enjoyed during the previous weeks. Which do they think their families and friends might like to try ?

Activity ideas:

- Make a minibeast trail, showing visitors where some interesting animals may be seen. Talk to the children about including a variety of minibeasts, high and low places, and perhaps some unexpected or special discoveries such as a beautiful spider's web behind a gatepost. Involve the children in making information labels with drawings, or the names of the minibeasts to be found. These labels will be placed around the trail to show visitors where to look.

- Make a camouflage treasure hunt. Hide a number of lengths of different coloured wool in an outside area. Some of the lengths of wool will be easily seen and some will be more difficult, depending on their colour and that of their background. Introduce the trail by explaining that the lengths of wool are tasty caterpillars and the children are hungry birds. How many caterpillars can they find? Which were the easiest to spot?

- Make a special reading corner containing stories and books relating to the topic. Invite visiting adults to be guest readers, enjoying a story, poetry, information or picture book with small groups of children. Encourage the children to pick out favourite books to share with their visitors.

- Make a minibeast world in the sand tray. Place some clean pebbles or smooth stones in the sand tray, a flower pot or two, a large piece of bark and some large leaves. Hide a number of plastic minibeasts under the objects and buried in the sand.

- Provide materials for children to help their guests in making their own minibeast hats and camouflage masks (see previous pages).

Making refreshments

- Let children decorate ladybird treats to serve to their guests. Cover round biscuits with ready-made fondant icing, coloured red. Provide tubes of black decorating jelly (available from supermarkets) and some chocolate drops of the type used in making cookies.

- Cut out sandwiches using a round biscuit cutter. Arrange in long rows on a bed of lettuce to form sandwich caterpillars. To each caterpillar add an eye made from a small piece of tomato and antennae and legs cut from cucumber strips.

- Make cheese pastry snails, by coiling strips of puff pastry. Use water to fix a pastry body to the shell and then sprinkle with grated cheese before baking.

Making posters

- Explain to the children that guests will need to know about their event. Discuss the types of information people might need - date, time, place, and so on. Write the text on a sheet of A4 paper and make several photocopies. Invite children to add their own minibeast illustrations to the poster designs and then photocopy enlargements if desired.

Join our minibeast trail

Resources

Resources to collect

- Pictures of minibeasts.
- Wrapping papers with minibeast designs.
- Magnifiers.
- Plastic minibeasts (toy shops).

Everyday resources

- Boxes, large and small, for modelling.
- Card cylinders from the centre of paper rolls.
- Papers and cards of different weights, colours and textures such as sugar paper, corrugated card, silver and shiny papers.
- Dry powder paints for mixing and mixed paints for covering large areas such as card tree trunks.
- Different sized paint brushes from household brushes to thin brushes for delicate work and a variety of paint mixing containers.
- A variety of drawing and colouring pencils, crayons, pastels, charcoals and chalks.
- Additional decorative and finishing materials such as sequins, foils, glitter, tinsel, shiny wool and threads, beads, pieces of textiles.
- Table covers.

Stories

If at First You Do Not See by Ruth Brown (Hippo Books, Scholastic Publications).

The Very Hungry Caterpillar by Eric Carle (Picture Puffins).

The Bad Tempered Ladybird by Eric Carle (Hamish Hamilton).

The Very Busy Spider by Eric Carle (Hamish Hamilton).

The Very Quiet Cricket by Eric Carle (Hamish Hamilton).

The Honey Bee and the Robber by Eric Carle (Philomel Books).

Molly and the Snorgle Fly by Satoshi Kambayashi (Tesco Books).

One Hungry Spider by Jeannie Baker (Andre Deutsch).

Mr Buzz the Beeman by Allan Ahlberg, *Happy Families* series (Puffin).

Ladybird Moves Home by Richard Fowler (Doubleday).

Honeybee's Busy Day by Richard Fowler (Doubleday).

Listen to this Story by Grace Hallworth (Magnet).

Poems

This Little Puffin by Elizabeth Matterson (Puffin).

Out and About by Shirley Hughes (Walker Books).

A First Poetry Book (Oxford University Press).

Non fiction

Caterpillar Caterpillar by Vivian French *Read and Wonder* series (Walker Books).

Spider Watching by Vivian French *Read and Wonder* series (Walker Books).

Incredible Minibeasts Christopher Maynard *Snapshot* series (Dorling Kindersley).

Butterfly, See How they Grow series (Dorling Kindersley).

How do Bees Make Honey? Usborne *Starting Point Science* (Usborne).

Snail by Jons Olesen *Stop Watch* series.

Ladybird by Barrie Watts *Stop Watch* series.

Songs

Eeny Meeny Minibeasts by David Moses in *Songs Compiled by Peter Morrell* in the *Collections* series (Scholastic).

Eighteen Spiders by David Moses in *Songs Compiled by Peter Morrell* in the *Collections* series (Scholastic).

The Ants go Marching in *Okki-tokki-unga* chosen by Beatrice Harrop, Linda Friend and David Gadsby (A & C Black.)

Collecting evidence of children's learning

Monitoring children's development is an important task. Keeping a record of children's achievements will help you to see progress and will draw attention to those who are having difficulties for some reason. If a child needs additional professional help, such as speech therapy, your records will provide valuable evidence.

Records should be the result of collaboration between group leaders, parents and carers. Parents should be made aware of your record keeping policies when their child joins your group. Show them the type of records you are keeping and make sure they understand that they have an opportunity to contribute. As a general rule, your records should form an open document. Any parent should have access to records relating to his or her child. Take regular opportunities to talk to parents about children's progress. If you have formal discussions regarding children about whom you have particular concerns, a dated record of the main points should be kept.

Keeping it manageable

Records should be helpful in informing group leaders, adult helpers and parents and always be for the benefit of the child. However, keeping records of every aspect of each child's development can become a difficult task. The sample shown will help to keep records manageable and useful. The golden rule is to keep them simple.

Observations will basically fall into three categories:

- **Spontaneous records:** Sometimes you will want to make a note of observations as they happen, for example a child is heard counting cars accurately during a play activity, or is seen to play collaboratively for the first time.

- **Planned observations:** Sometimes you will plan to make observations of children's developing skills in their everyday activities. Using the learning opportunity identified for an activity will help you to make appropriate judgements about children's capabilities and to record them systematically.

To collect information:

- talk to children about their activities and listen to their responses;

- listen to children talking to each other;

- observe children's work such as early writing, drawings, paintings and 3D models. (Keeping photocopies or photographs is sometimes useful.)

Sometimes you may wish to set up 'one off' activities for the purposes of monitoring development. Some groups, for example, ask children to make a drawing of themselves at the beginning of each term to record their progressing skills in both co-ordination and observation. Do not attempt to make records following every activity!

- **Reflective observations:** It is useful to spend regular time reflecting on the progress of a few children (about four each week). Aim to make some brief comments about each child every half term.

Informing your planning

Collecting evidence about children's progress is time consuming and it is important that it is useful. When you are planning, use the information you have collected to help you to decide what learning opportunities you need to provide next for children. For example, a child who has poor pencil or brush control will benefit from more play with dough or construction toys to build the strength of hand muscles.

Example of recording chart

Name: Daisy Bentley			D.O.B. 26.2.96		Date of entry: 13.9.99	
Term	**Personal and Social**	**Language and Literacy**	**Mathematics**	**Knowledge and Understanding**	**Physical**	**Creative**
ONE	Reluctant to say good bye to mother. Prefers adult company 20.11.99 EMH	Enjoys listening to stories. 'Hungry Caterpillar' a favourite 20.11.99 EMH	Is able to say numbers to ten and count accurately five objects. Recognises and names squares and circles. 5.12.99 BM	Very keen on minibeasts Brought in pictures from home 16.10.99 AC	Can balance on one leg. Finds threading beads difficult. 16.10.99 AC	Enjoys gluing and cutting. Made a wonderful Duplo castle 20.10.99 LSS
TWO						
THREE						

Skills overview of six week plan

Week	Topic focus	Personal and Social	Language and Literacy	Mathematics	Knowledge and Understanding of the World	Physical	Creative
1	Meet the minibeasts!	Safety Being sensitive towards animals	Talking Sequencing Initial sounds Prepositions	Describing size Counting	Observing Describing; Sorting	Moving with confidence imagination & awareness of space	Listening Role play Collaborative building
2	Creep and crawl	Awareness of feelings	Action rhymes Initial sounds Extending vocabulary	Number rhyme Exploring measure	Looking at materials; Observing Describing	Balancing Using malleable materials Moving imaginatively	Modelling Responding to music
3	Hum and buzz	Awareness of feelings Sharing ideas Working collaboratively	Extending vocabulary Initial sounds Listening	Counting Awareness of larger numbers; Shape	Constructing Comparing Observing	Miming Aiming Fielding	Finger painting Weaving
4	Flutter and fly	Awareness of feelings; Sensitivity to others	Rhyme and sounds; Writing names; Telling stories	Symmetry Matching; Early measuring; Counting	Awareness of living things Joining	Using malleable materials Moving with imagination & awareness of space	Collage Dancing Using materials
5	Weave and spin	Sharing ideas Discussing feelings	Making predictions Rhymes; Listening	Counting Comparing measure	Observing; Knowledge of living things; Investigating; Constructing	Role play Aiming; Moving with awareness of space	Weaving Marble rolling Making
6	Minibeast world	Discussing ideas Working collaboratively	Talking Responding Listening	Measuring Counting	Discussing places Observing	Action rhymes Moving with imagination	Modelling

Planning for Learning through Minibeasts

Home links

The theme of Minibeasts lends itself to useful links with children's homes and families. Through working together children and adults gain respect for each other and build comfortable and confident relationships.

Establishing partnerships

- Keep parents informed about the topic of Minibeasts, and the themes for each week. By understanding the work of the group, parents will enjoy the involvement of contributing ideas, time and resources.

- Photocopy the parent's page for each child to take home.

- Invite friends, childminders and families to share all or part of the Minibeast World event.

Visiting enthusiasts

- Ask at the local library for the names of any bee keeping associations in the area whose members may be willing to come into the group to show artefacts or talk about their interest. Specialists in

natural history from museums are often willing to talk to groups, or an enthusiast from a gardening club may have a particular knowledge of garden wildlife. Conservation groups are also a useful source of minibeast experts.

Resource requests

- Ask parents to contribute any fabric scraps, buttons, ribbons, trimmings or parcel decorations which are no longer needed.

- Photographs of minibeasts, birthday cards or wrapping papers with minibeast designs will all be useful.

Preparing the event

- It is always useful to have extra adults at events, and support in preparing food will be especially welcome.